All rights reserved. No part of this book may be reproduced or used in any manner without written permission of the copyright owner except for the use of quotations in a book review.

Copyright © 2021 by Kristen Dovnik

Designed in Australia.

What could I see?

Created by
Kristen Dovnik

What could I see on a Farm?

- Rainbow
- Sky
- Cloud
- Fence
- Tractor
- Farmer
- Plum Tree
- Cows
- Calf
- Chickens
- Chicks
- Rooster
- Mower
- Rabbits
- Grass
- Corn
- Pig
- Piglets
- Vegetable Garden

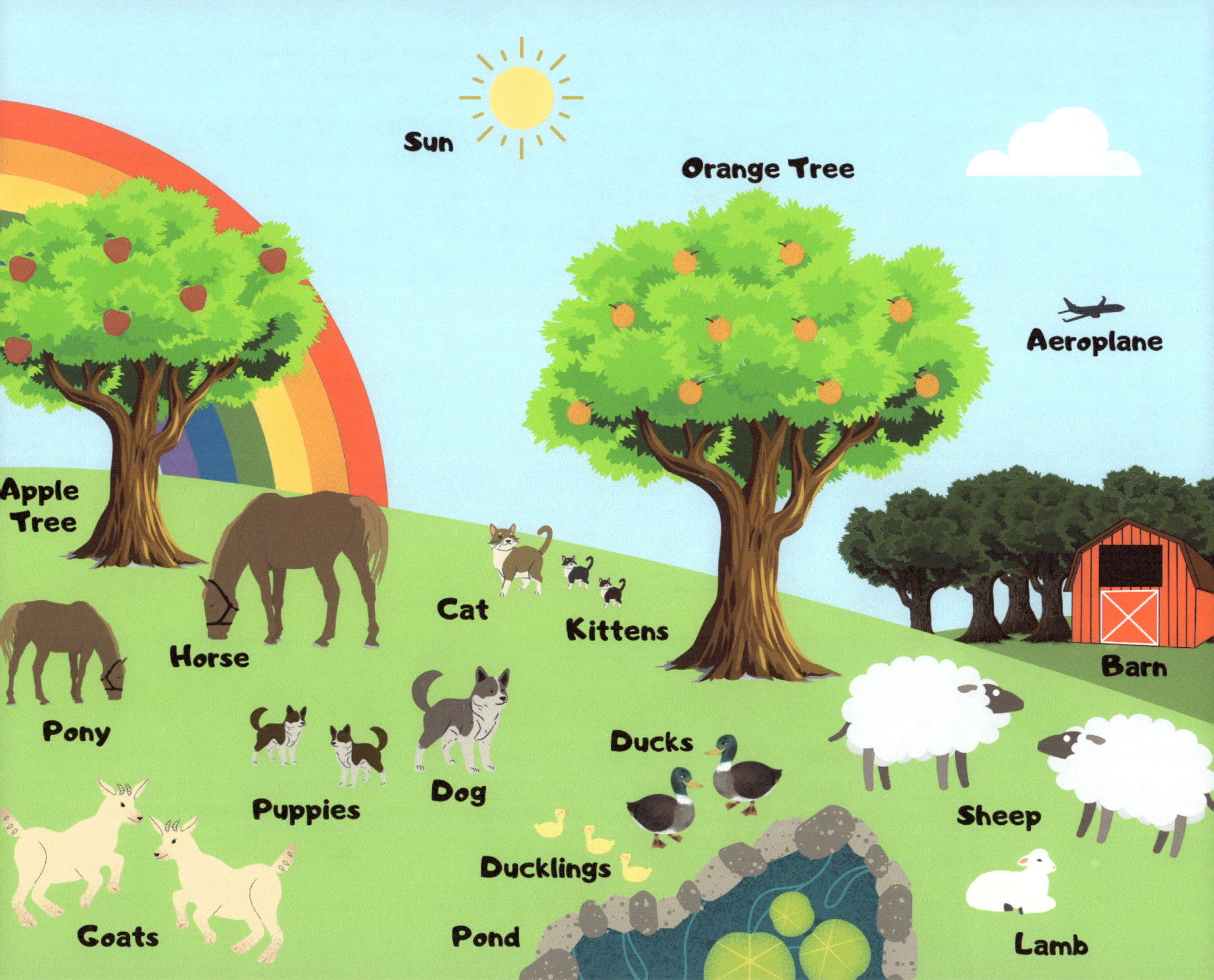

What could I see in the wild?

Sunset
Eagle
Monkey
Toucan
Hippo
Water
Orangutan
Giraffe
Zebra
Crocodile
Tiger
Elephant Cub
Flowers
Elephant
Frog
Fox
Lioness
Leopard
Cheetah
Cub
Rhino
Lion

What could I see in the Ocean?

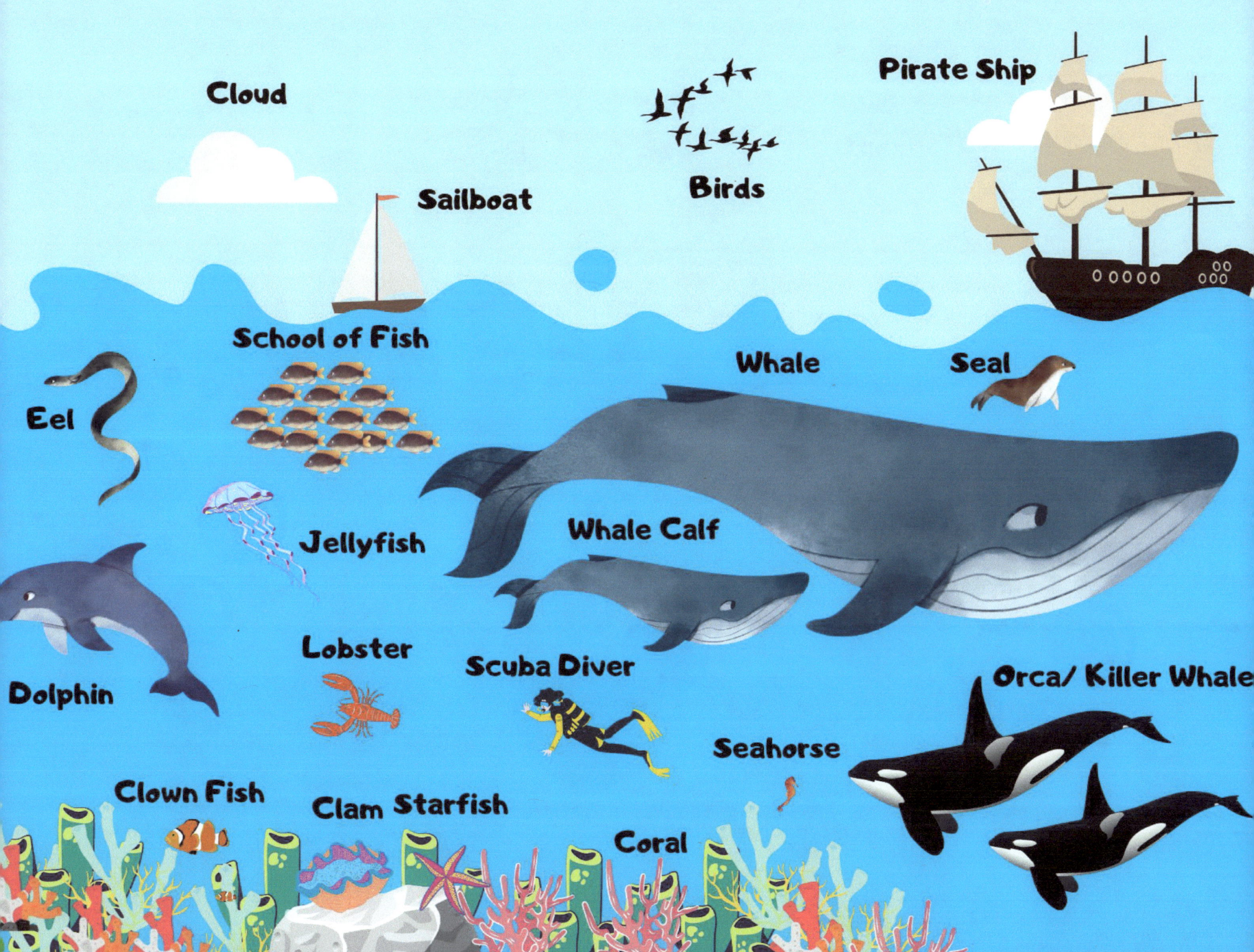

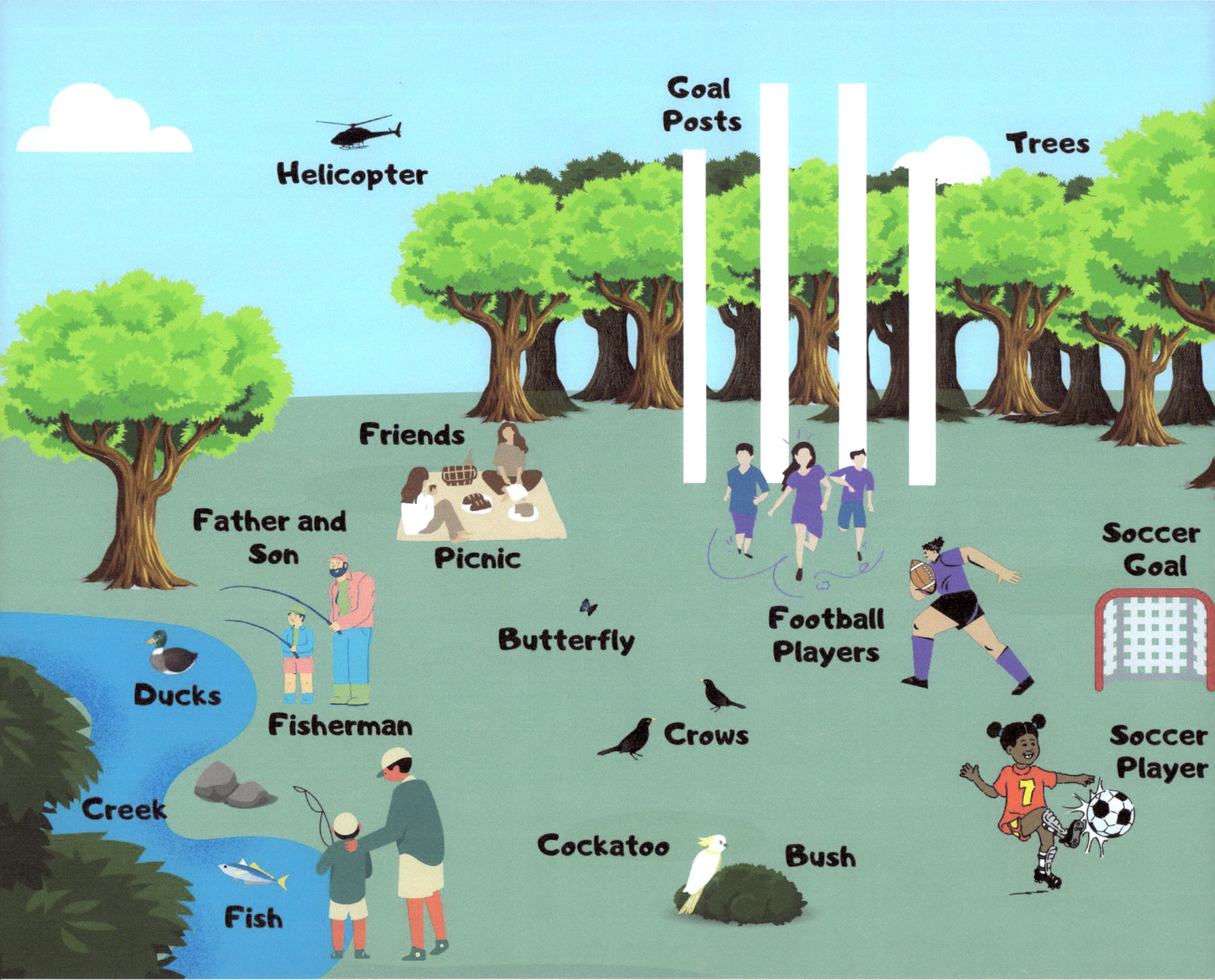

What could I see in Outer Space?

Space Station

Moon

Meteor

Mercury

Venus

Satellite

Constellation

Sun

Asteroids

Earth

What could I see at the Beach?

Shark Fin
Lighthouse
Red and Yellow Flags
Swimmers
Lifeguard Tower
Shells
Kayak
Starfish
Kids
Life Jacket
Goggles
Warning Sign
Flippers
Shovel
Bathers
Surfboard
Lifebuoy
Lifeguard

More books by Kristen Dovnik

Everyday ABC's For Toddlers

Created by Kristen Dovnik

www.ingramcontent.com/pod-product-compliance
Lightning Source LLC
Chambersburg PA
CBHW050853010526
44107CB00047BA/1601